In the same series by PatrickGeorge:

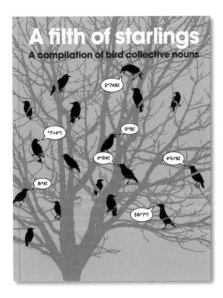

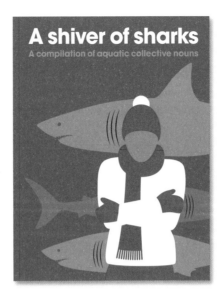

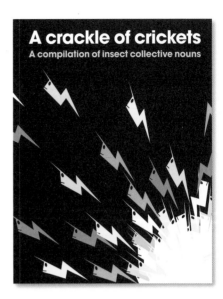

© PatrickGeorge 2012
Second edition revised
First published in the United Kingdom in 2009

Illustrated, designed and published by
PatrickGeorge
46 Vale Square
Ramsgate
Kent CT11 9DA
United Kingdom

www.patrickgeorge.biz

ISBN 978-1-908473-03-5

British Library Cataloguing in Publication Data.
A catalogue record for this book is available from the British Library.

Printed in China.

A drove of bullocks

A compilation of animal collective nouns

PatrickGeorge

A tower of giraffes

The giraffe towers above the rest of us, being the tallest
animal in the world. If danger is near, it will break into a 35-mile
an hour run and protecting its young, can kill a lion with a
kick of its front hooves. Using the giraffe as an early warning
system, other grassland animals will graze nearby to feel safe.

A kennel of dogs

It seems that we become more and more dotty over our canine companions: they share our homes, even our bedrooms, some go to the hairdresser and some are dressed in fashionable items. From collars to jumpers, T-shirts to hoodies, the kennel is no longer top of the shopping list!

A crash of rhinoceroses

When rhinos fight, they crash their horns together but the horns are not just used for fighting, they are also used for guiding their young and pushing dung into piles to mark their territory. The black and the white rhino are actually a shade of grey with different facial characteristics and habitats.

An implausibility of gnus

This ungainly animal of awkward appearance is an implausibly fast runner, able to reach up to 50 miles an hour in an effort to avoid its many predators. Every year, it becomes one of nature's finest spectacles – migrating northwards in herds of up to 1.5 million. An incredible sight!

A dazzle of zebras

Why zebras have stripes is baffling. No two zebras have identical
stripes and it is not clearly apparent why they have them.
A dazzling mirage of black and white in the heat of the sun,
the zebra could easily confuse its predators, yet it is thought that
their unique stripes also help individuals identify one another.
Baffled and dazzled we may be – this creature is one of a kind.

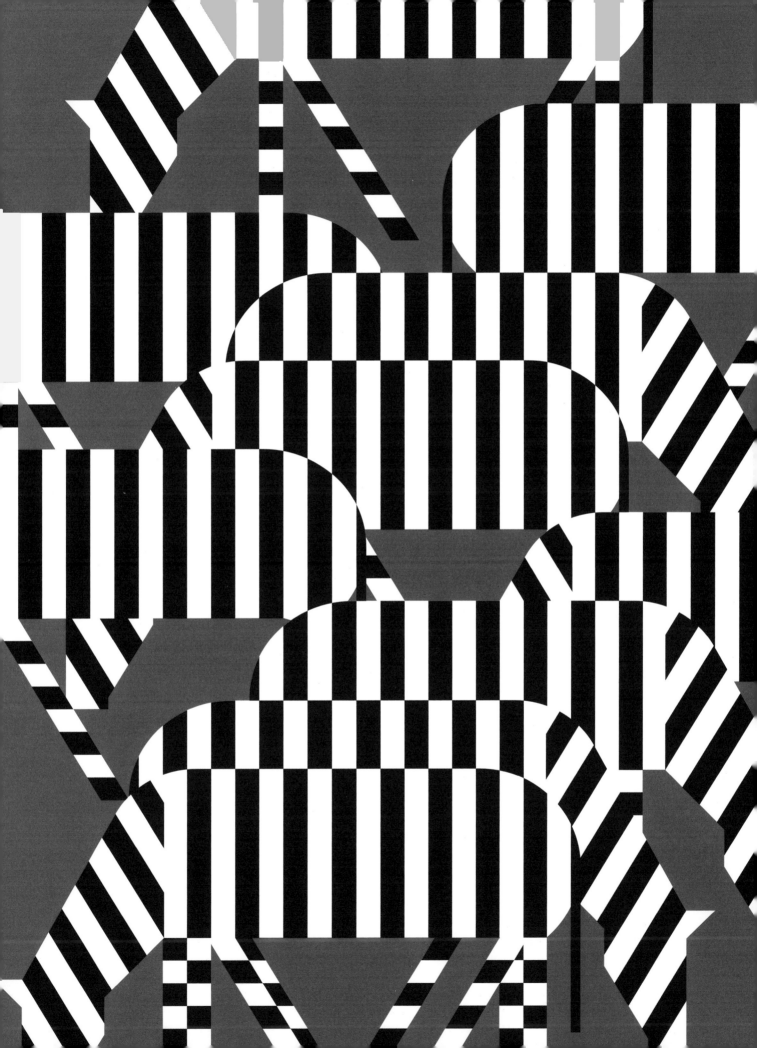

An embarrassment of pandas

With few giant pandas left in the world and about
10 per cent of their population in zoos, we stand a better
chance these days of seeing a panda in captivity than
in the wild. Naturally a solitary animal, this much-loved
bear is on show to thousands of visitors every year.

A parade of elephants

Whatever its role, this animal has every reason to blow its own trumpet. Powerful yet gentle, patient and loyal, and capable of great affection to its family or its keeper, this striking animal is widely revered. During festivals in Asia, they are adorned with colourful accessories and form an essential part of the parade.

A pride of lions

Proud to be the only member of the cat family to live
in a pride and proud to own an impressive mane,
the king of the jungle will laze around during the day.
Regal though it may be, it lets itself down by squabbling
over a kill or stealing food from other animals.

A quiver of cobras

You may quiver when you see a cobra but in fact the cobra is just as likely to recoil when it sees you. A shy reptile that avoids human contact at all costs, it will rear up aggressively and either spit its venom or kill you with a single bite. And you will quiver no more.

A mob of meerkats
The mob works together in groups of about thirty, carefully organised and with one member always on the lookout. At the slightest scent of danger the alarm is raised and the gang quickly disperses to the safety of its burrow and out of harm's way.

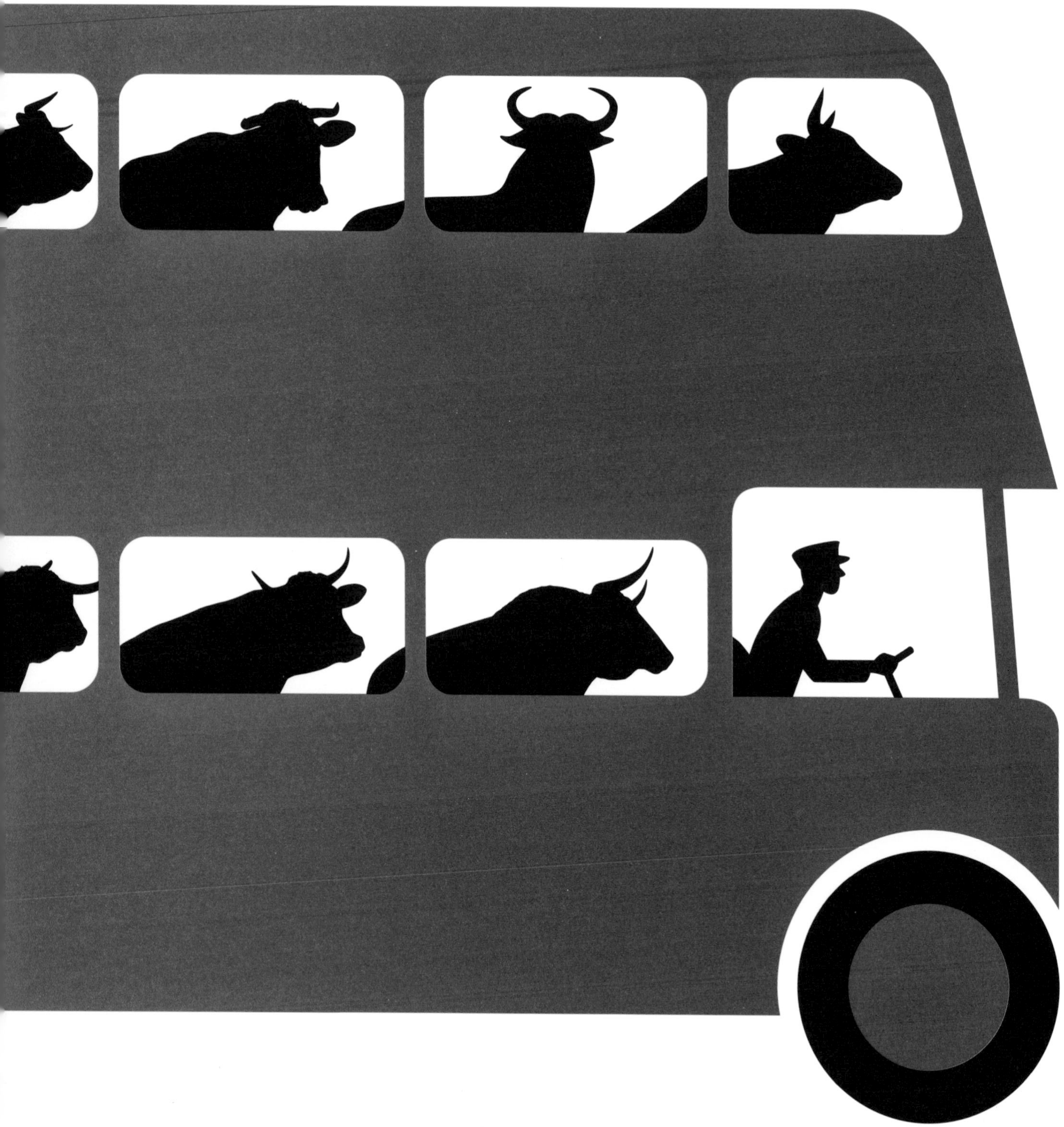

A drove of bullocks

Also known as steers or oxen, they work as a team
pulling and drawing, helping drive transport and
machinery. Often ploughing, hauling, trampling, they
can work twenty at one time or simply in pairs. People
born under the influence of the Ox are kind, logical,
positive, and with their feet firmly planted on the ground.

A parcel of hogs

The term 'hog' can denote a person who is greedy,
dirty or selfish, yet the pig is intelligent and gentle. With
its keen sense of smell it is used for foraging for truffles,
its skin used for leather and its bristles for brushes.
Add in some pancetta to make a fine parcel of goods!

A band of gorillas

The amazing Western gorilla is the world's largest primate. Despite its fearsome appearance, it is a shy and quiet animal that lives in small bands of 1-2 males, several females and their young. The male gorilla will grow until it is 12 years old when it develops a saddle of silvery white hair on its back, giving it the name 'silverback'.

A train of camels
Beasts of burden, these animals have been used in the Sahara for thousands of years. Commonly used for fetching and carrying cargo, the hardy camel train will travel miles a day in seemingly inhospitable conditions. A robust means of transportation, they also provide desert communities with meat, wool, milk and fuel.

A gaze of raccoons

The North-American raccoon, with its distinctive black mask and intelligent gaze, is on the lookout for food just about anywhere. It adapts easily to any environment and, using its long fingers and dexterous paws, it can open and eat pretty much whatever it fancies.

A litter of kittens

In some countries kittens are treated as litter – often
unwanted and disposed of quite freely. Not many,
however, can resist the appeal of the cute, cuddly kitten
and a kitten in the home will soon adopt you as its surrogate
mother, purring, kneading and trusting. If a cat rolls over
to display its belly, this indicates a feeling of total security.

A skulk of foxes

It hunts mostly at night, skulking around bins and farmyards. Urban and wild, the red fox is cunning and resourceful and uses its hunting skills to catch a wide variety of prey. One of nature's survivors.

A business of ferrets

This active sleuth prefers to snoop about at dawn and dusk, sleeping between 14 and 18 hours during the day. Upon waking, it likes to run about and leap in exuberant play before getting down to business. Although it has a short attention span, it can be trained to 'ferret' out rabbits through a system of repetitive rewards.

A pace of donkeys

The cutely affectionate, patient, persistent donkey operates at a steady pace, reassuring young foals or nervous horses and fiercely protecting those it has bonded with. An intelligent animal with a keen sense of survival, it will not do anything it deems dangerous but freezes when threatened as taking flight will get it nowhere.

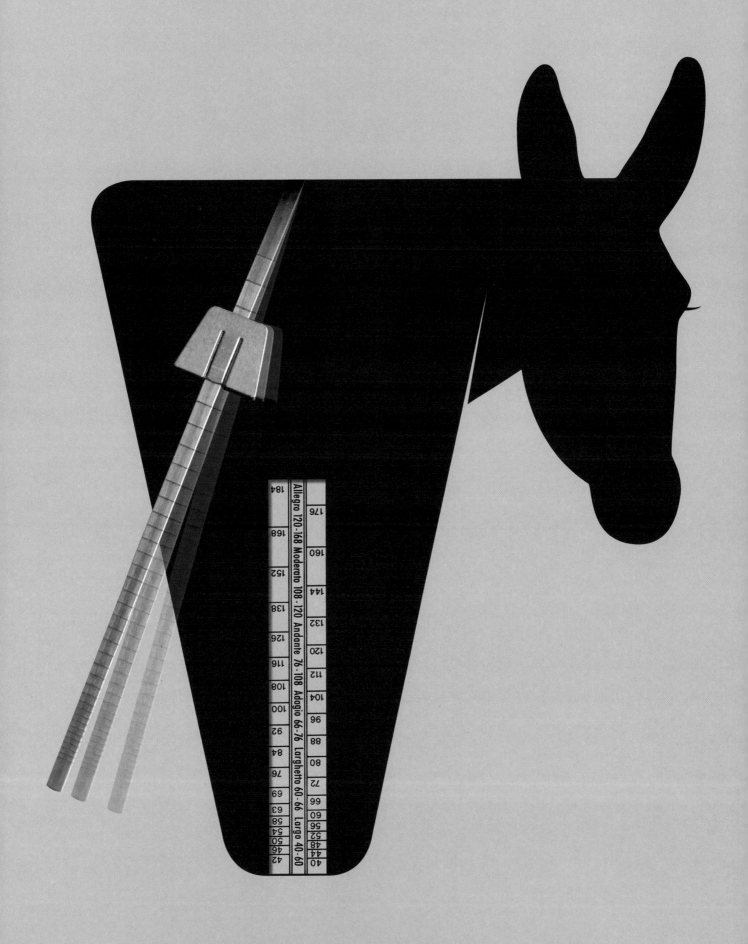

A cloud of bats

Gregarious by nature and living together in their thousands, a black cloud of bats emerge from their roost every evening in search of food. Most rely on echolocation to find insects whilst others use a keen sense of smell and night vision, in search of fruit and flowers.